jinx
and heavenly
calling

Kelly Dunlar

LILY POETRY REVIEW BOOKS

Deep in a life is another life.

~ Marianne Boruch

yins

and heavenly

calling.

For

me?

Table of Contents

under a spell

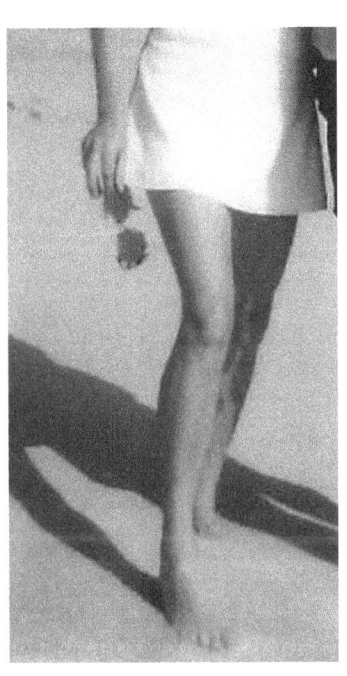

to court

pardon
>   poor penmanship
in bed

to appear
Superior

do a bit
of hurrying.

summons

good salesman

Here I am again.
to stay

try 2 a day
I go fast

    you should have
    the finished product

by summer

    only kidding
    3 weeks

I can pep you up
            flourescent

Our little "rush"

such good
"vitamins."

breathe
like flying.

I'm in a bad

way

hopping and dashing

sticking neck out

heart tricked

under a spell

and fetching

strange trip

tomorrow ~~little~~

I would have died

Back to the dull

settle

Then

surprise

weak minded?

I didn't behave myself

I've rambled

your plans for

the great fun

pushing me up the mountain

is how it will end

"first site"

a tour through Blue
Tomorrow

     crack of dawn
     to chase you

Thanksgiving
I shall not drink my downfall

dress rehearsal

week-ends
worth the head cold—

trouble
may grow

fast—make
heart & soul
a party

afterwards

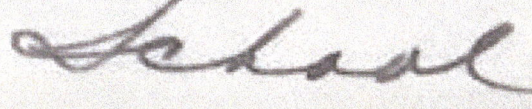

the big plunge

dreamed I could

how to move

strong and broad

to cry for such charming *give up*

etc. for

no doubt you are

hard? thinking *the "right man"*

of me, you haunt

    I can think of worse

to wait to drop

into bed

joker

eyes open to fight

      I practiced wonder

ful tremendous fling

      my kiss   shock

everyone—awfully

      let us

shrewd the hour

      I will arrive

do you want me

      so tell me do you

I'll fight my way into

      difficult seeings

mischief

I like you "little bit" "big
bit"

                won't have my
                foot

fixed until you sang to me

would be bedfellow

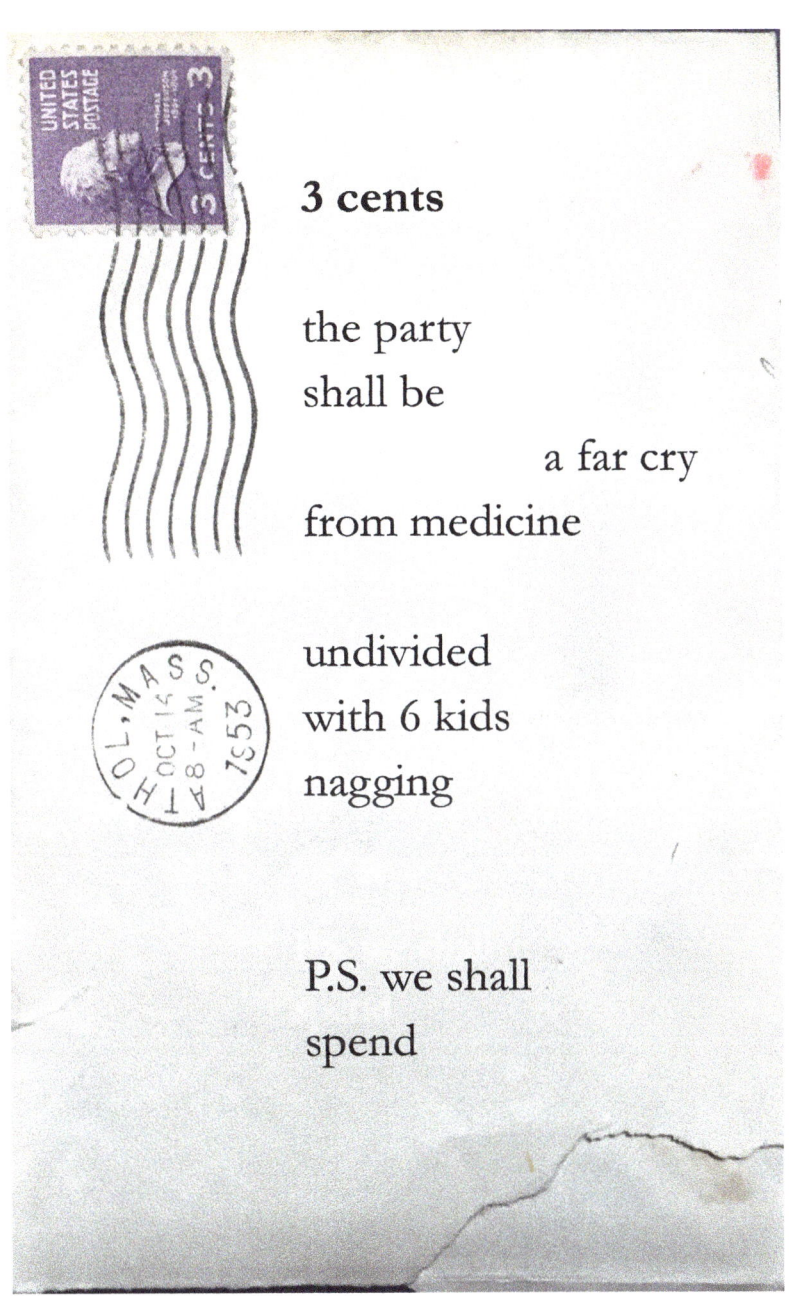

3 cents

the party
shall be
                    a far cry
from medicine

undivided
with 6 kids
nagging

P.S. we shall
spend

whew! what a day!

10:00 a.m.

hard to believe
unless you see

4:00

now!
be my sacrifice

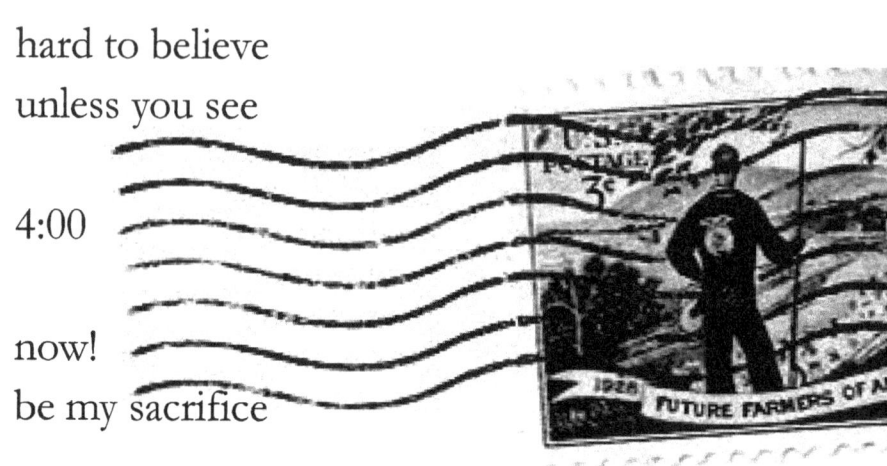

you don't have
too much rest
of your life

I'm spoiled too!

I'll have my "motherly
complex" and besides

tonight
I'm so talented

tomorrow
I'll close

— _I like ya_

mad spring!
can't save a cent

we dashed
the cost

well worth it

to finish your
lonesome

     don't feel me
     don't sound me

     "befuddled" me

things are cooking
80-81-86-81

give me an appetite, Lord!
eating my masterpiece

even my brother said tale

I am!
a "catch"

single so long
smells burned

the terms

ever work to get real of you that
now that there is a button messing,

for the sweater

---

you will never

get back

as stated I

will find one

sew it on

keep it

electric

morning came

quickly

for which I am sorry—extroverts

go off and leave me to make

my own fun until I am spoiled

in "The happiest"

extremely happy now.

my lovely trophy

I want you   stubbornness   dash

& permanent

Honey trouble

Sleep to dream of you
    I dream and when I do

You last in the world

hurt and truly
for liquor so wild   *can't promise*

forget as you may be able   *I'll try.*

hopes high   *counting*
sneak out the days

storm

around

the corner

hectic the ladies

and party a party
tomorrow.

you'll have to

revive me

be nice

when you can

forewarn

Shirley

going down
back to bump
embarrassed

best to warn you
but so far too sharp

and sad to be sharpened
enough for my muscles
after each terrific

foolish neck

on the way to church
                    frozen death

Instead went sliding
*how I flew
so fast when I was
slippery*

but what a long walk
back up pulling a blast

of dynamite

Jackpot

moody more so
frightened

no fear

have faith to keep *spend it*
a handsome caddy

to do all the "racy"

Wishes

Thoughts
all
Good

chance

we'll try our
sport

skating a great between
"16" pregnancies

    clown! I raise you
I'm loaded, lucky

too   too
  cracking
typing
    improving

plugging a woman's never
a dull evening

go a blizzard

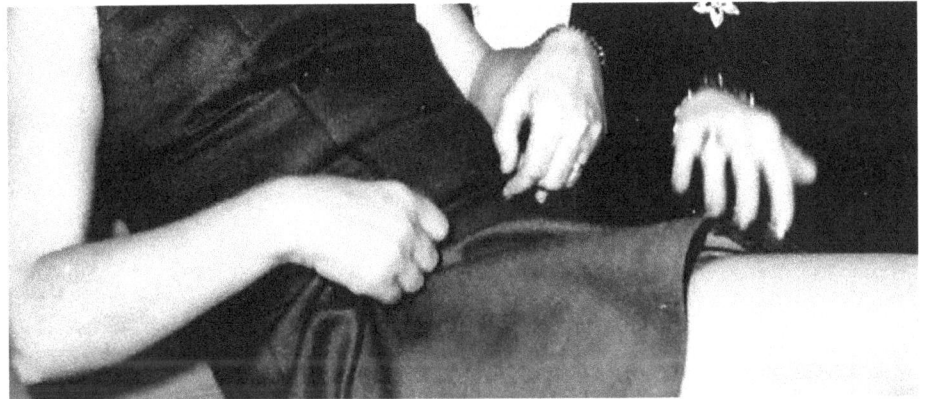

spree

use it up

don't care what

come too early

be too much

better

get every color

worry the scales

dash sleep circles

under my eyes

sacrifice

ends together

    and will make
    you for a son
    lucky

all nite all day

maneuvering

Dr. tomorrow

is painful

    Strapped up.

I got a bang

about the bed

    really a riot

before my "gala"

come back stage

    if you're game

just a note

I'm still alive

in my cold

cold

bed

snow

ready to drop a riot

finished back
started front

maybe we'll fit
together

      after yarn

I'm embarrassed for room
to romp

      but I can afford
to go a blizzard

cartoons

your chances are
girl standing on ledge

my chances hope
to wear you out

men—some
never tip-top

report sorta weak
after the bout with envy

the weight I lost
put my father bankrupt

I'll be bells on
into the floating

will power

for once

                    I'd love to be bad

better to find

the "man in my life"

                    have them all Happy

the brownies so handy

love isn't your throat

                    catching

one thing wrong I did to my hair

polish a ring to run

                    for me to happen

to you

much and then

lost your way?

all the beautiful beautiful once

more tickets, send tickets get tickets terrific

did you ever get washed?

come out and season

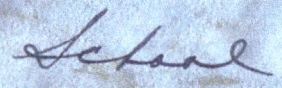

long as you wear

rather late

faithful, elegant and naturally
I ate

my share, cocktails
cold down, hit the

Hog Back as
housework

dish pan hands
all better

tomorrow is knit

be not as fast
to the highways

to travel alone

I purchased

the horrible if only
I was rich and
rich off my legs

not pregnant according
to you 9/12 of the year

good honey writing
pleased to hear compliments

you're only one throat

go down and give devil
the streets are tomorrow

slippery
relish my measurements

especially tricks
I, not being a bashful

soul to be advertised
blackmail me

don't know what you want
start with the feet

slip & bra, skirt, blouse
cover it all

remember figures

It's private! darn new born
Gosh cute!

don't stop writing honey

take me now

mother in the distant
always

36

hectic

fire fire fire fire

ripping between

a sleigh ride

a downslide

which one of us

would resist

a crying

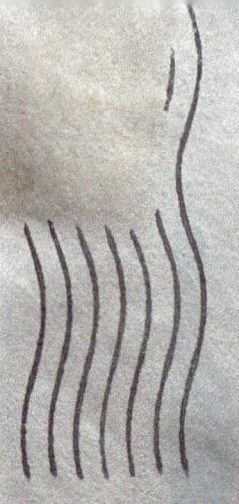

weight

who eats
happy in love

quite an armful
of losing

tease

    a picture
    a pin-up
    to fix it

in vain

weakened
eat honey

beware!!!

look

to the future

look helped if I'd had 2 strong
wrap around me

awful

lonesome

to get married

it's slippery

the size of it.

     the size of kids

     to all day stay

     home & baby

the size of it.   sit.

     probably   Oops

the size of it.   time is faster

     dash now

our share

party among
mischief

cute   will mean more
after cake, before

we starve death

valentine

there's

a cloud

where we are

too late to make

amends

Honey for supper

I'm green with thought

for ages scrape someday

gone   long

no sign of a period

chance caught up

goodness

smart beautiful

instead of brilliant
need a drink

dare a bad accident
dare a "bed time"

Oh yes—fireworks
like rain soon

afterwards

mother snuck
behind me

took rear view
payment of dues

possible

children

eat worry
give scare

Sneak
a better
anywhere

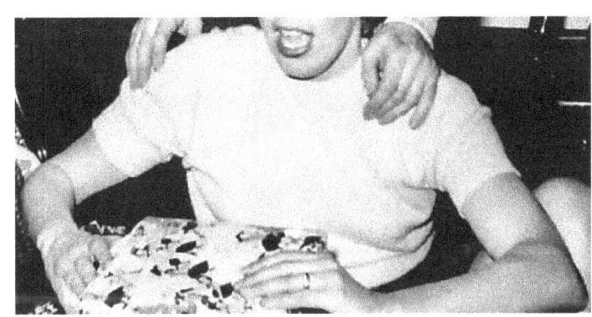

b a b i e d

Received   this
absolutely   physical

                   putting.   decided

grown up

      before
      diplomatic doctors
      question my funny awful

      I have a million
      presents

      buy out

                        free time

knowing

A psychiatrist surrounded
   women an hour a week
a nut job

   get out sick
    find   instead
    party switch

sneak a better
anywhere

mother, father

mend a spring
wedding if all
goes probably
     burlap sack
     in the same boat
     best wash
the white out
soak to "good
news"

insurance

amounts to   stashed

away   rainy

not least

top secret

chances

what   schedule is

tomorrow

Lake

awake   nites   walk
balcony

keep crickets
company

summer come
listen

after married

murder sound
sleeper

*shall let you explore it with me as
your personal guide. O. K?*

worry

your folks

                    my folks

children brought

up protestant   washed

like   a woodsman

         instead

of a   businessman

What horrible

         season

is iron

        and doubt

in the world coming

finish laundry

talk honey

begin to bill

a bit of money

deduct from   sooner

                      or later   be

unafraid for best   salary

be like a diamond

mounted and million

fly by

day will brave

the first tell all

~~rig~~ ring   cast   pull

~~nec~~essary ends

the best parents

know the worst
                    point blank
fact

                    correct   error
                    welcome. etc.

(immediate family
that ring   full
of questions!

57

dumps

leave selfish before

spoil

terrible

horrible

spoil

& blue

for being

worry.

sensible

trouble &

love

dope.

"ours"

pray all the days
and   keeping

eat   enjoy
but   knowing

makes the   nausea

wonder
as   possible

be "tight" with
sleep & lucky

get the   available
priest   be   glad

you'd like. — you probably would like

feeding "two"

eat fat

in heavens name   more

pile more   than necessary

not to sacrifice

as much   as possible

till then

Tuesday

Dusty

flashy

stationery

thrifty

marry

honey

sorry

"secretary"

a pretty suit

worn dresses have loads
of Ha!

time flies—forever!

Mm was it good

all
short &
sweet luck

Easter Parade

picture a riot
Telegram tomorrow

sad news should wear
your wedding dress

dark suits worn
by groom in a semi-church

Easters for all now
new after cleaners

snug

loaf
laundry
shirts
exams
silver
sewing
you

likewise

father
    having
mother

father
    wedding
mother

weaken blue gown & pink
    gown

charge plate pick
    luck

ages

cartoon

cute

happiest _____

easy

clubs

Bridal

blue gown

pink gown

charge plate

exam

Gamble

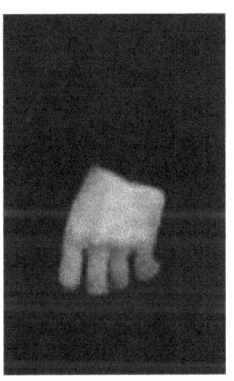

"skinny fingers"

ring   mother wants
me to wear

hers   I need
a guard

for the setting
          non-Catholic

telling the turn

say anything under
troubled intentions

children   light
definite

to church

hope

                gone sinus

sharp need
fresh   air

a few called the priest
a good fellow with pamphlets

put stock in   might
& Gamble

                father   briefly
constantly changes

1 day

weather lasts until
you believe it

be nervous not in the least

know children say badly
about everyone wonderful

mistake each other
be first in heart and children next

tickets don't forget

mock wedding

glow easier

all friends started on nothing
made out—a lot

father shall know   time
mother bring   don't forget

Masquers riot
Electric Pop-up

call fiddle   to play   Best of luck

"husband"

we're all widows in the "flesh"

elevate the pelvic
never out of bed medi-cine

Dr. Have you gotten our lamp
fixed yet?

jinx and heavenly   calling
Mrs. - that's you

hard to get
used to

junior

Have you decided
yet whether or not

you'll want
and let me

survive
the rough

Mrs. *miss me a little*

arrived to an empty

all day + *all nite.*
stomach ached

feel so fat—look so

married   *wife*

      hand wasn't

      my own

      your key

      in your blue pants

washed machine sweet

surprise

misunderstanding

do anything
up to a certain
point

drive one way
or the other

camp the rest

Afterword

poach—to take without permission and use as one's own

This collection is crafted from words I poached from the pages of handwritten letters from my mother to my father, 1953-1954. She was twenty-six years old, living with her parents in Athol, Massachusetts, working as a records librarian at the local hospital. My father was living as a boarder in a house on Fresh Pond Parkway, Cambridge, Massachusetts, while attending the Harvard Business School. They knew each other in high school, as casual friends, and graduated from the same class in 1942. Here's how they were described by their classmates in their yearbook:

"Jokes Are the Joy Of Life"

Swish!! There she was hustling to her next class. Yes, that was Brack, always in a rush and bubbling over with tales to tell. She was one of the majorettes for the band, and many a day you saw her strut down the field after a victorious football game. She was an active member of the school paper and was known as the girl you like to have around.

Activities: Senior play; Usher, Junior Prom; Marshal, Graduation III; Majorette III, IV; L. R. S. II, III, IV; Girls Sports I, II, III, IV; Usher, Senior Prom.

"Giggles"

Blonde, handsome Dusty never gave the girls much of a break, as he was more interested in hockey during the winter. As soon as spring broke, however, he was at the golf course. He was very popular and was elected president of the Student Council in his senior year. Outside of school he was an active member of the Christian Endeavor during his high school years.

Activities: President Student Council; Chairman, Classbook Committee; Football III, IV; Hockey I, III, IV; Senior Play; Usher, Senior Prom.

The letters were saved by his mother, Flora, in her Athol home, in a cardboard box. I received the letters from my older brother who can't remember exactly how they came into his possession. Some time after Flora's death he found them in his basement. I do not know if Flora read her daughter-in-law's letters. As far as I know, aside from my father, I am the only one who has read my mother's letters in their entirety. The originals have not been harmed in the making of this book.

I have poached the letter writer's original words, taken them out of context, and created my own imaginary world. The poems are what I plucked and shaped as my eye scanned down the page spontaneously selecting words and phrases—by instinct, by hunger, by intuition, by mischief, by choice, by whimsy—to create what Mary Ruefle calls "a poetic experience."

Notes on Form

I borrowed ideas on form from erasure poets, and made up these rules I followed
in creating this collection: One letter per poem. Many of the letters consist of
multiple pages. Sometimes I selected only from the first page or the second page,
or from all pages. However, I could only select words working forward through the
letter, never backward. So the selected words and punctuation appear in the order
made in the original letter. I followed the original use of capitalisation. If the word
was capitalised in the letter, it appears capitalised in the poem. Original spelling is
preserved. Punctuation was selected in the same way as the words. If I wanted
to use a comma, period, question mark, etc., it had to appear in the letter, follow-
ing the rules of order. The palimpsest, or visual background, on which each poem
is set, is made from the original letter or its envelope. Some, but not all, of the
letters were preserved with their envelopes.

Acknowledgements

Snug, 3 cents, Our little "rush" and *Wishes,* published in *Thimble*, April 2022

hectic and *Skinny fingers* published in *Glint*, December 2022

dress rehearsal, to be published in *Fifty Plus Advocate,* April 2023

The quote from Marianne Boruch's poem "Nest" first appeared in her book *A Stick That Breaks and Breaks,* © 1997 by Oberlin College, and is reprinted by permission of Oberlin College Press.

Special thanks to the members of Tom Daley's Monday night poetry group who generously responded to this work in process over the course of many months: Tom Daley, Jenny Grassl, Eileen Cleary, Paul Nemser, Gale Batchelder, Robert Carr, Mid Walsh, Catherine Morocco, Robin Linn and Talia Pinzari. Without their astute craft suggestions, inspiration and encouragement, this book would not have taken shape.

About Kelly DuMar

My mother gave birth to me on October 26, 1958 at Athol Memorial Hospital where she had worked as a records librarian until marrying my father in May 1954. I am one of five children born to my parents between 1955 and 1964. I am the middle child, born third, between two girls and two boys. My mother's first pregnancy in 1954 ended in miscarriage after their marriage.

My parents lived together until my mother's death in 2008 in their home in Sherborn, Massachusetts in a house they bought when I was three months old. My father sold the Sherborn home and returned, briefly, to live in Athol before his death in 2018.

For the past twenty years, I have lived on the Charles River, in Sherborn, Massachusetts, with my husband. Our three adult children and grandson return often to our home in these woods on the banks of the Charles—habitat of my writing life.

www.ingramcontent.com/pod-product-compliance
Lightning Source LLC
Chambersburg PA
CBHW051640120626
46551CB00014B/2157